# This Journal Belongs To:

_____

Journal Ideas For Everyone

# Weekly Agenda

| | |
|---|---|
| MON | |
| TUE | |
| WED | |
| THUR | |
| FRI | |
| SAT | |
| SUN | |

# Weekly Planner

## TASKS & ERRANDS

**MON:**

**TUES:**

**WED:**

**THUR:**

**FRI:**

**SAT:**

**SUN:**

## TO DO LIST:

## NOTES & REMINDERS

THOUGHTS

# Daily Planner

DATE

MORNING:

TOP PRIORITIES:

AFTERNOON:

APPOINTMENTS:

EVENING:

NOTES:

GOALS FOR THE DAY::

# Daily Planner

DATE

TOP PRIORITIES:

APPOINTMENTS:

GOALS FOR THE DAY::

MORNING:

AFTERNOON:

EVENING:

NOTES:

# Daily Planner

DATE

MORNING:

TOP PRIORITIES:

AFTERNOON:

EVENING:

APPOINTMENTS:

NOTES:

GOALS FOR THE DAY::

# Daily Planner

DATE

_____

TOP PRIORITIES:

MORNING:

AFTERNOON:

APPOINTMENTS:

EVENING:

NOTES:

GOALS FOR THE DAY::

# Daily Planner

DATE

MORNING:

_____

TOP PRIORITIES:

AFTERNOON:

EVENING:

APPOINTMENTS:

NOTES:

GOALS FOR THE DAY::

# Daily Planner

DATE

_____

TOP PRIORITIES:

APPOINTMENTS:

GOALS FOR THE DAY::

MORNING:

AFTERNOON:

EVENING:

NOTES:

# My Action Plan

DATE:

## TOP PRIORITIES

## GOALS

ACTION STEPS       STATUS      ✔

MILESTONES & REWARDS:

THOUGHTS & REFLECTIONS::

# Checklist

FOR: _____     DATE: _____     ✓

_____     _____
_____     _____
_____     _____
_____     _____
_____     _____
_____     _____
_____     _____
_____     _____
_____     _____
_____     _____
_____     _____
_____     _____
_____     _____

NOTES:

# Notes

# Weekly Agenda

| | |
|---|---|
| MON | |
| TUE | |
| WED | |
| THUR | |
| FRI | |
| SAT | |
| SUN | |

# Weekly Planner

| TASKS & ERRANDS |
|---|
| **MON:** |
| **TUES:** |
| **WED:** |
| **THUR:** |
| **FRI:** |
| **SAT:** |
| **SUN:** |

## TO DO LIST:

## NOTES & REMINDERS

THOUGHTS

# Daily Planner

DATE

_____

TOP PRIORITIES:

APPOINTMENTS:

GOALS FOR THE DAY::

MORNING:

AFTERNOON:

EVENING:

NOTES:

# Daily Planner

DATE
_____

TOP PRIORITIES:

APPOINTMENTS:

GOALS FOR THE DAY::

MORNING:

AFTERNOON:

EVENING:

NOTES:

# Daily Planner

DATE

_____

MORNING:

TOP PRIORITIES:

AFTERNOON:

EVENING:

APPOINTMENTS:

NOTES:

GOALS FOR THE DAY::

# Daily Planner

DATE

TOP PRIORITIES:

APPOINTMENTS:

GOALS FOR THE DAY::

MORNING:

AFTERNOON:

EVENING:

NOTES:

# Daily Planner

DATE

_____

TOP PRIORITIES:

APPOINTMENTS:

GOALS FOR THE DAY::

MORNING:

AFTERNOON:

EVENING:

NOTES:

# Daily Planner

DATE

_____

TOP PRIORITIES:

APPOINTMENTS:

GOALS FOR THE DAY::

MORNING:

AFTERNOON:

EVENING:

NOTES:

# My Action Plan

DATE:

## TOP PRIORITIES

## GOALS

| ACTION STEPS | STATUS | ✔ |
|---|---|---|
| | | |
| | | |
| | | |
| | | |

MILESTONES & REWARDS:

THOUGHTS & REFLECTIONS::

# Checklist

FOR:                                    DATE:                          ✓

# Notes

# Weekly Agenda

| | |
|---|---|
| MON | |
| TUE | |
| WED | |
| THUR | |
| FRI | |
| SAT | |
| SUN | |

# Weekly Planner

## TASKS & ERRANDS

**MON:**

**TUES:**

**WED:**

**THUR:**

**FRI:**

**SAT:**

**SUN:**

## TO DO LIST:

## NOTES & REMINDERS

THOUGHTS

# Daily Planner

DATE

_____

TOP PRIORITIES:

MORNING:

AFTERNOON:

APPOINTMENTS:

EVENING:

NOTES:

GOALS FOR THE DAY::

# Daily Planner

DATE

TOP PRIORITIES:

APPOINTMENTS:

GOALS FOR THE DAY::

MORNING:

AFTERNOON:

EVENING:

NOTES:

# Daily Planner

DATE

_____

TOP PRIORITIES:

APPOINTMENTS:

GOALS FOR THE DAY::

MORNING:

AFTERNOON:

EVENING:

NOTES:

# Daily Planner

DATE
_____

TOP PRIORITIES:

MORNING:

AFTERNOON:

APPOINTMENTS:

EVENING:

NOTES:

GOALS FOR THE DAY::

# Daily Planner

DATE

MORNING:

TOP PRIORITIES:

AFTERNOON:

EVENING:

APPOINTMENTS:

NOTES:

GOALS FOR THE DAY::

# Daily Planner

DATE

MORNING:

TOP PRIORITIES:

AFTERNOON:

APPOINTMENTS:

EVENING:

NOTES:

GOALS FOR THE DAY::

# My Action Plan

DATE:

TOP PRIORITIES

GOALS

ACTION STEPS

STATUS ✔

MILESTONES & REWARDS:

THOUGHTS & REFLECTIONS::

# Checklist

FOR: _____         DATE: _____         ✓

_____

_____

_____

_____

_____

_____

_____

_____

_____

_____

_____

_____

_____

_____

NOTES:

# Notes

# Weekly Agenda

| | |
|---|---|
| MON | |
| TUE | |
| WED | |
| THUR | |
| FRI | |
| SAT | |
| SUN | |

# Weekly Planner

| TASKS & ERRANDS |
|---|
| **MON:** |
| **TUES:** |
| **WED:** |
| **THUR:** |
| **FRI:** |
| **SAT:** |
| **SUN:** |

## TO DO LIST:

## NOTES & REMINDERS

THOUGHTS

# Daily Planner

DATE

_____

TOP PRIORITIES:

APPOINTMENTS:

GOALS FOR THE DAY::

MORNING:

AFTERNOON:

EVENING:

NOTES:

# Daily Planner

DATE

TOP PRIORITIES:

APPOINTMENTS:

GOALS FOR THE DAY::

MORNING:

AFTERNOON:

EVENING:

NOTES:

# Daily Planner

DATE

TOP PRIORITIES:

APPOINTMENTS:

GOALS FOR THE DAY::

MORNING:

AFTERNOON:

EVENING:

NOTES:

# Daily Planner

DATE
_____

TOP PRIORITIES:

MORNING:

AFTERNOON:

APPOINTMENTS:

EVENING:

NOTES:

GOALS FOR THE DAY::

# Daily Planner

DATE
_____

TOP PRIORITIES:

APPOINTMENTS:

GOALS FOR THE DAY::

MORNING:

AFTERNOON:

EVENING:

NOTES:

# Daily Planner

DATE

_____

MORNING:

TOP PRIORITIES:

AFTERNOON:

EVENING:

APPOINTMENTS:

NOTES:

GOALS FOR THE DAY::

# My Action Plan

DATE:

## TOP PRIORITIES

## GOALS

## ACTION STEPS

## STATUS ✔

## MILESTONES & REWARDS:

## THOUGHTS & REFLECTIONS::

# Checklist

FOR:                                    DATE:                          ✓

NOTES:

# Notes

# Weekly Agenda

| | |
|---|---|
| MON | |
| TUE | |
| WED | |
| THUR | |
| FRI | |
| SAT | |
| SUN | |

# Weekly Planner

| TASKS & ERRANDS |
|---|
| **MON:** |
| **TUES:** |
| **WED:** |
| **THUR:** |
| **FRI:** |
| **SAT:** |
| **SUN:** |

## TO DO LIST:

## NOTES & REMINDERS

THOUGHTS

# Daily Planner

DATE

_____

TOP PRIORITIES:

MORNING:

AFTERNOON:

EVENING:

APPOINTMENTS:

NOTES:

GOALS FOR THE DAY::

# Daily Planner

DATE

_____

TOP PRIORITIES:

APPOINTMENTS:

GOALS FOR THE DAY::

MORNING:

AFTERNOON:

EVENING:

NOTES:

# Daily Planner

DATE

_____

MORNING:

TOP PRIORITIES:

AFTERNOON:

EVENING:

APPOINTMENTS:

NOTES:

GOALS FOR THE DAY::

# Daily Planner

DATE

_____

TOP PRIORITIES:

APPOINTMENTS:

MORNING:

AFTERNOON:

EVENING:

NOTES:

GOALS FOR THE DAY::

# Daily Planner

DATE

_____

TOP PRIORITIES:

APPOINTMENTS:

GOALS FOR THE DAY::

MORNING:

AFTERNOON:

EVENING:

NOTES:

# Daily Planner

DATE

_____

TOP PRIORITIES:

APPOINTMENTS:

GOALS FOR THE DAY::

MORNING:

AFTERNOON:

EVENING:

NOTES:

# My Action Plan

DATE:

## TOP PRIORITIES

## GOALS

## ACTION STEPS

STATUS ✔

## MILESTONES & REWARDS:

## THOUGHTS & REFLECTIONS::

# Checklist

FOR: _____      DATE: _____      ✓

_____

_____

_____

_____

_____

_____

_____

_____

_____

_____

_____

_____

_____

_____

NOTES:

# Notes

# Weekly Agenda

| MON | |
|-----|--|
| TUE | |
| WED | |
| THUR | |
| FRI | |
| SAT | |
| SUN | |

# Weekly Planner

## TASKS & ERRANDS

**MON:**

**TUES:**

**WED:**

**THUR:**

**FRI:**

**SAT:**

**SUN:**

## TO DO LIST:

## NOTES & REMINDERS

THOUGHTS

# Daily Planner

DATE

_____

MORNING:

TOP PRIORITIES:

AFTERNOON:

EVENING:

APPOINTMENTS:

NOTES:

GOALS FOR THE DAY::

# Daily Planner

DATE
_____

TOP PRIORITIES:

APPOINTMENTS:

GOALS FOR THE DAY::

MORNING:

AFTERNOON:

EVENING:

NOTES:

# Daily Planner

DATE

_____

MORNING:

TOP PRIORITIES:

AFTERNOON:

EVENING:

APPOINTMENTS:

NOTES:

GOALS FOR THE DAY::

# Daily Planner

DATE

_____

TOP PRIORITIES:

APPOINTMENTS:

GOALS FOR THE DAY::

MORNING:

AFTERNOON:

EVENING:

NOTES:

# Daily Planner

DATE

TOP PRIORITIES:

APPOINTMENTS:

MORNING:

AFTERNOON:

EVENING:

NOTES:

GOALS FOR THE DAY::

# Daily Planner

DATE
_____

TOP PRIORITIES:

APPOINTMENTS:

GOALS FOR THE DAY::

MORNING:

AFTERNOON:

EVENING:

NOTES:

# My Action Plan

DATE:

## TOP PRIORITIES

## GOALS

## ACTION STEPS

## STATUS

✔

## MILESTONES & REWARDS:

## THOUGHTS & REFLECTIONS::

# Checklist

FOR:                              DATE:                    ✓

NOTES:

# Notes

# Weekly Agenda

| | |
|---|---|
| MON | |
| TUE | |
| WED | |
| THUR | |
| FRI | |
| SAT | |
| SUN | |

# Weekly Planner

| TASKS & ERRANDS |
|---|
| **MON:** |
| **TUES:** |
| **WED:** |
| **THUR:** |
| **FRI:** |
| **SAT:** |
| **SUN:** |

## TO DO LIST:

## NOTES & REMINDERS

THOUGHTS

# Daily Planner

DATE
_____

MORNING:

TOP PRIORITIES:

AFTERNOON:

EVENING:

APPOINTMENTS:

NOTES:

GOALS FOR THE DAY::

# Daily Planner

DATE

_____

TOP PRIORITIES:

MORNING:

AFTERNOON:

APPOINTMENTS:

EVENING:

NOTES:

GOALS FOR THE DAY::

# Daily Planner

DATE

MORNING:

TOP PRIORITIES:

AFTERNOON:

EVENING:

APPOINTMENTS:

NOTES:

GOALS FOR THE DAY::

# Daily Planner

DATE

_____

TOP PRIORITIES:

APPOINTMENTS:

MORNING:

AFTERNOON:

EVENING:

NOTES:

GOALS FOR THE DAY::

# Daily Planner

DATE

TOP PRIORITIES:

APPOINTMENTS:

GOALS FOR THE DAY::

MORNING:

AFTERNOON:

EVENING:

NOTES:

# Daily Planner

DATE

MORNING:

TOP PRIORITIES:

AFTERNOON:

EVENING:

APPOINTMENTS:

NOTES:

GOALS FOR THE DAY::

# My Action Plan

DATE:

## TOP PRIORITIES

## GOALS

## ACTION STEPS

STATUS ✔

MILESTONES & REWARDS:

THOUGHTS & REFLECTIONS::

# Checklist

FOR:                          DATE:                    ✓

NOTES:

# Notes

# Weekly Agenda

| | |
|---|---|
| **MON** | |
| **TUE** | |
| **WED** | |
| **THUR** | |
| **FRI** | |
| **SAT** | |
| **SUN** | |

# Weekly Planner

| TASKS & ERRANDS |
| --- |
| **MON:** |
| **TUES:** |
| **WED:** |
| **THUR:** |
| **FRI:** |
| **SAT:** |
| **SUN:** |

## TO DO LIST:

## NOTES & REMINDERS

THOUGHTS

# Daily Planner

DATE

_____

TOP PRIORITIES:

APPOINTMENTS:

GOALS FOR THE DAY::

MORNING:

AFTERNOON:

EVENING:

NOTES:

# Daily Planner

DATE

_____

TOP PRIORITIES:

APPOINTMENTS:

GOALS FOR THE DAY::

MORNING:

AFTERNOON:

EVENING:

NOTES:

# Daily Planner

DATE

_____

TOP PRIORITIES:

APPOINTMENTS:

GOALS FOR THE DAY::

MORNING:

AFTERNOON:

EVENING:

NOTES:

# Daily Planner

DATE

_____

MORNING:

TOP PRIORITIES:

AFTERNOON:

EVENING:

APPOINTMENTS:

NOTES:

GOALS FOR THE DAY::

# Daily Planner

DATE

_____

TOP PRIORITIES:

APPOINTMENTS:

GOALS FOR THE DAY::

MORNING:

AFTERNOON:

EVENING:

NOTES:

# Daily Planner

DATE

_____

MORNING:

TOP PRIORITIES:

AFTERNOON:

EVENING:

APPOINTMENTS:

NOTES:

GOALS FOR THE DAY::

# My Action Plan

DATE:

## TOP PRIORITIES

## GOALS

## ACTION STEPS

## STATUS                    ✔

## MILESTONES & REWARDS:

## THOUGHTS & REFLECTIONS::

# Checklist

FOR:                                    DATE:                              ✓

NOTES:

# Notes

# Weekly Agenda

| | |
|---|---|
| MON | |
| TUE | |
| WED | |
| THUR | |
| FRI | |
| SAT | |
| SUN | |

# Weekly Planner

## TASKS & ERRANDS

**MON:**

**TUES:**

**WED:**

**THUR:**

**FRI:**

**SAT:**

**SUN:**

## TO DO LIST:

## NOTES & REMINDERS

THOUGHTS

# Daily Planner

DATE

_____

TOP PRIORITIES:

APPOINTMENTS:

GOALS FOR THE DAY::

MORNING:

AFTERNOON:

EVENING:

NOTES:

# Daily Planner

DATE

_____

TOP PRIORITIES:

MORNING:

AFTERNOON:

APPOINTMENTS:

EVENING:

NOTES:

GOALS FOR THE DAY::

# Daily Planner

DATE
_____

MORNING:

TOP PRIORITIES:

AFTERNOON:

EVENING:

APPOINTMENTS:

NOTES:

GOALS FOR THE DAY::

# Daily Planner

DATE

_____

TOP PRIORITIES:

MORNING:

AFTERNOON:

EVENING:

APPOINTMENTS:

NOTES:

GOALS FOR THE DAY::

# Daily Planner

DATE

_____

TOP PRIORITIES:

APPOINTMENTS:

GOALS FOR THE DAY::

MORNING:

AFTERNOON:

EVENING:

NOTES:

# Daily Planner

DATE

_____

TOP PRIORITIES:

APPOINTMENTS:

GOALS FOR THE DAY::

MORNING:

AFTERNOON:

EVENING:

NOTES:

# My Action Plan

DATE:

## TOP PRIORITIES

## GOALS

## ACTION STEPS

STATUS ✔

MILESTONES & REWARDS:

THOUGHTS & REFLECTIONS::

# Checklist

FOR:

DATE:

✓

NOTES:

# Notes

# Notes

# Notes

# Notes

# Notes

# Notes

Made in the USA
Monee, IL
17 April 2022